If you use this book...

Amazon offers you a wide range of papers that are carefully manufactured for colored pencils and alcohol-based markers to guarantee you flawless results. To maintain the quality of your artistic creations when using wet media, it is strongly recommended to place a sheet of paper under the page you are painting. This prevents possible bleeding, keeping your artwork immaculate.

We are grateful that...

you have decided to start a coloring journey with us, and sincerely hope that every page brings you joy and relaxation.

If you find pleasure in bringing these pages to life, we would be delighted if you share your experiences and leave a review on Amazon. Your insights are invaluable in improving not only our work but also the experiences of future artists like you. Your contribution to our creative community is truly appreciated. Thank you for coloring the world with us.

This book belongs to

Colour Test Page

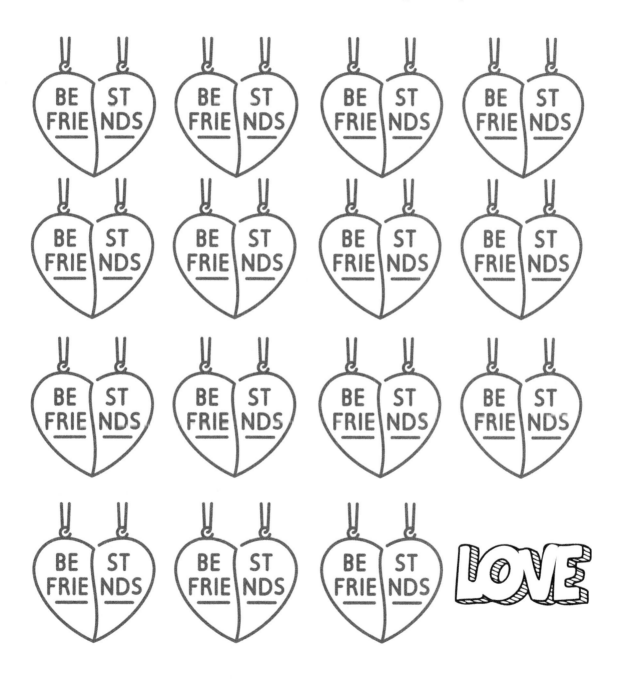

Printed in Great Britain
by Amazon

60012420R00054